T. McElligott

P9-DTR-510

by W· H· AUDEN

EPISTLE
TO A GODSON

and Other Poems

W·H·AUDEN

EPISTLE
TO A GODSON
and Other Poems

RANDOM HOUSE   NEW YORK

ISBN: 0:394-48203-4

Library of Congress Catalog Card Number: 72-1428

The following poems appeared originally in *The New Yorker: Moon Landing, The Art of Healing, The Aliens, A Shock,* and *Talking to Myself.*

Some of these poems have appeared in *The New York Review of Books, Harper's, The Scientific American, Poetry, The New Statesman, London Magazine, Isis.*

Manufactured in the United States of America by The Book Press, Brattleboro, Vermont

24689753

FIRST EDITION

for ORLAN FOX

Each year brings new problems of Form and Content
new foes to tug with: at Twenty I tried to
vex my elders, past Sixty it's the young whom
      I hope to bother.

CONTENTS

EPISTLE
TO A GODSON
and Other Poems

EPISTLE TO A GODSON

for PHILIP SPENDER

DEAR PHILIP: "Thank God for boozy godfathers"
you wrote in our guest-book, which was flattering:
    though I've reached the years when discretion
    calls for a yearly medical check-up,

who am I to avouch for any Christian
baby, far less offer ghostly platitudes
    to a young man? In yester times it
    was different: the old could still be helpful

when they could nicely envisage the future
as a named and settled landscape their children
    would make the same sense of as they did,
    laughing and weeping at the same stories.

Then sheep and goats were easy to recognize,
local fauna: good meant Giles the shoemaker
    taking care of the village ninny,
    evil Count ffoulkes who in his tall donjon

indulged in sinister eccentricities.
But *I speak from experience,* how could I
 say that to you, who can't remember
 when everyone travelled by railway,

and the poor were what they were used to being,
the creators of wealth not, as now they are,
 an expensive nuisance? (Nobody
 has dared suggest gassing them, but someone

surely will.) You don't need me to tell you what's
going on: the ochlocratic media,
 joint with under-the-dryer gossip,
 process and vent without intermission

all to-day's ugly secrets. Imageable
no longer, a featureless anonymous
 threat from behind, to-morrow has us
 gallowed shitless: if what is to happen

occurs according to what Thucydides
defined as "human," we've had it, are in for
 a disaster that no four-letter
 words will tardy. I've beheld in nightmares

(who hasn't?) likely abominations: seething
behavioral sinks, the Muses scuttering,
 smelly, from eutrophied Helicon,
 the Witches Sabbath on Garbage Mountain,

Herod's genetic engineers commanded
to modify the Innocents. By then, with
 any luck, the tangible Me should
 be mineral, too set in my habits

4

to distinguish light from darkness, and valued
in current prices as three-dollars-fifty:
      but you might well be there, if what is
      ripely is not promptly done. Yet who can

issue proper instructions? Not, certainly,
our global Archons, whose top-lofty slogans
      are as off the beam as their syntax
      is vague: (they would be figures of fun, if

very clever little boys had not found it
amusing to build devices for them, more
      apt at disassembly than any
      old fire-spewing theogonic monster.)

To be responsible for the happiness
of the Universe is not a sinecure:
      in elite lands your generation
      may be called to opt for a discipline

that out-peers the monks, a Way of obedience,
poverty and—good grief!—perhaps chastity,
      yet in this world's ill-weathered open,
      a stern venture pre-figured in folk-tales

as the Quest Perilous. For such wayfarers,
what should we write to give them the nourishment,
      warmth and shelter they'll be in need of?
      Nothing obscene or unpleasant: only

the unscarred overfed enjoy Calvary
as a verbal event. Nor satiric: no
      scorn will ashame the Adversary.
      Nor shoddily made: to give a stunning

display of concinnity and elegance
is the least we can do, and its dominant
mood should be that of a Carnival.
Let us hymn the small but journal wonders

of Nature and of households, and then finish
on a serio-comic note with legends
of ultimate eucatastrophe,
regeneration beyond the waters.

But perhaps you think poems are as foolish
as most poets, and would rather spend your spare
moments romping around in Cantor's
logical paradise, or beseeching

such knotty points as *Can we hang a robber
who is not there?* or *What is the color of
the number Three?* Why not? All pleasures
come from God. Since I *am* your godfather,

I'll close this letter with some worldly maxims:
*Be glad your being is unnecessary,
then turn your toes out as you walk, dear,
and remember who you are, a Spender.*

THE ART OF HEALING

IN MEMORIAM DAVID PROTETCH, M.D.

Most patients believe
dying is something they do,
        not their physician,
        that white-coated sage,
never to be imagined
        naked or married.

        Begotten by one,
I should know better. "Healing,"
        Papa would tell me,
        "is not a science,
but the intuitive art
        of wooing Nature.

        Plants, beasts, may react
according to the common
        whim of their species,
        but all humans have
prejudices of their own
        which can't be foreseen.

To some, ill-health is
a way to be important,
        others are stoics,
        a few fanatics,
who won't feel happy until
        they are cut open."

        Warned by him to shun
the sadist, the nod-crafty,
        and the fee-conscious,
        I knew when we met,
I had found a consultant
        who thought as he did,

        yourself a victim
of medical engineers
        and their arrogance,
        when they atom-bombed
your sick pituitary
        and over-killed it.

        "Every sickness
is a musical problem,"
        so said Novalis,
        "and every cure
a musical solution":
        You knew that also.

        Not that in my case
you heard any shattering
        discords to resolve:
        to date my organs
still seem pretty sure of their
        self-identity.

For my small ailments
you, who were mortally sick,
        prescribed with success:
        my major vices,
my mad addictions, you left
        to my own conscience.

        Was it your very
predicament that made me
        sure I could trust you,
        if I were dying,
to say so, not insult me
        with soothing fictions?

        Must diabetics
all contend with a nisus
        to self-destruction?
        One day you told me:
"It is only bad temper
        that keeps me going."

        But neither anger
nor lust are omnipotent,
        nor should we even
        want our friends to be
superhuman. Dear David,
        dead one, rest in peace,

        having been what all
doctors should be, but few are,
        and, even when most
        difficult, condign
of our biassed affection
        and objective praise.

9

LINES TO DR. WALTER BIRK
ON HIS RETIRING
FROM GENERAL PRACTICE

When you first arrived in Kirchstetten, trains had
long been taken for granted, but electric
light was still a surprise and as yet no one
    had seen a tractor.

To-day, after forty-five years, as you leave us,
autobahns are a must, mid-wives are banished,
and village doctors become museum pieces
    like the horse-and-buggy.

I regret. The specialist has his function,
but, to him, we are merely banal examples of
what he knows all about. The healer I faith is
    someone I've gossipped

and drunk with before I call him to touch me,
someone who admits how easy it is to misconster
what our bodies are trying to say, for each one
    talks in a local

dialect of its own that can alter during
its lifetime. So children run high fevers on
slight provocation, while the organs of old men
        suffer in silence.

When summer plumps again, our usual sparrows
will phip in the eaves of the patulous chestnuts
near your old home, but none will ask: "Is Doctor
        Birk around to hear me?"

For nothing can happen to birds that has not
happened before: we though are beasts with a sense of
real occasion, of beginnings and endings,
        which is the reason

we like to keep our clocks punctual as Nature's
never is. Seasons She has but no Calendar:
thus every year the strawberries ripen
        and the autumn crocus

flares into blossom on unpredictable
dates. Such a *Schlamperei* cannot be allowed an
historian: with us it's a point of honor
        to keep our birth-days

and wedding-days, to rejoice or to mourn, on
the right one. Henceforth, the First of October
shall be special for you and us, as the Once when
        you quit the Public

Realm to private your ways and snudge in a quiet
you so deserve. Farewell, and do not wince at
our sick world: it is genuine in age to be
        happily selfish.

A NEW YEAR GREETING

(After an Article by Mary J. Marples in The Scientific American,
Jan. 1969)

for VASSILY YANOWSKY

On this day tradition allots
        to taking stock of our lives,
my greetings to all of you, Yeasts,
        Bacteria, Viruses,
Aerobics and Anaerobics:
        A Very Happy New Year
to all for whom my ectoderm
        is as Middle-Earth to me.

For creatures your size I offer
        a free choice of habitat,
so settle yourselves in the zone
        that suits you best, in the pools
of my pores or the tropical
        forests of arm-pit and crotch,
in the deserts of my fore-arms,
        or the cool woods of my scalp.

Build colonies: I will supply
        adequate warmth and moisture,
the sebum and lipids you need,
        on condition you never
do me annoy with your presence,
        but behave as good guests should,
not rioting into acne
        or athlete's-foot or a boil.

Does my inner weather affect
        the surfaces where you live?
Do unpredictable changes
        record my rocketing plunge
from fairs when the mind is in tift
        and relevant thoughts occur
to fouls when nothing will happen
        and no one calls and it rains.

I should like to think that I make
        a not impossible world,
but an Eden it cannot be:
        my games, my purposive acts,
may turn to catastrophes there.
        If you were religious folk,
how would your dramas justify
        unmerited suffering?

By what myths would your priests account
    for the hurricanes that come
twice every twenty-four hours,
    each time I dress or undress,
when, clinging to keratin rafts,
    whole cities are swept away
to perish in space, or the Flood
    that scalds to death when I bathe?

Then, sooner or later, will dawn
    A Day of Apocalypse,
when my mantle suddenly turns
    too cold, too rancid, for you,
appetising to predators
    of a fiercer sort, and I
am stripped of excuse and nimbus,
    a Past, subject to Judgement.

SMELT AND TASTED

The nose and palate never doubt
Their verdicts on the world without,
But instantaneously condemn
Or praise each fact that reaches them:
Our tastes may change in time, it's true,
But for the fairer if they do.

Compared with almost any brute,
Our savouring is less acute,
But, subtly as they judge, no beast
Can solve the mystery of a feast,
Where love is strengthened, hope restored,
In hearts by chemical accord.

HEARD AND SEEN

Events reported by the ear
Are soft or loud, not far or near,
In what is heard we only sense
Transition and impermanence:
A bark, a laugh, a rifle-shot,
These may concern us or may not.

What-has-been and what-is-to-be
To vision form a unity:
The seen hill stays the way it is,
But forecasts greater distances,
And we acknowledge with delight
A so-on after every sight.

I AM NOT A CAMERA

Photographable life is always either trivial or already sterilised.

To call our sight Vision
implies that, to us,
all objects are subjects.

*   *   *

What we have not named
or beheld as a symbol
escapes our notice.

*   *   *

We never look at two people
or one person twice
in the same way.

*   *   *

It is very rude to take close-ups and, except
when enraged, we don't:
lovers, approaching to kiss,
instinctively shut their eyes before their faces
can be reduced to
anatomical data.

*   *   *

17

Instructive it may be to peer through lenses:
each time we do, though, we should apologise
to the remote or the small for intruding
upon their quiddities.

*   *   *

The camera records
visual facts: i.e.,
all may be fictions.

*   *   *

Flash-backs falsify the Past:
they forget
the remembering Present.

*   *   *

On the screen we can only
witness human behavior:
Choice is for camera-crews.

*   *   *

The camera may
do justice to laughter, but must
degrade sorrow.

A BAD NIGHT

(A lexical exercise)

In his dream zealous
To attain his home,
But ensorcelling powers
Have contorted space,
Odded the way:
Instead of a facile
Five-minute trot,
Far he must hirple,
Clumsied by cold,
Buffeted often
By blouts of hail
Or pirries of rain,
On stolchy paths
Over glunch clouds,
Where infrequent shepherds,
Sloomy of face,
Snudge of spirit,
Snoachy of speech,
With scaddle dogs

19

Tend a few scrawny
Cag-mag sheep.

Fetched into conscience
By a hoasting fit,
He lies darkling,
Senex morosus,
Too ebb of verve
Even to monster
Social trifles,
Or violent over
The world's wrongs,
While time drumbles,
A maunder of moments,
Wan, haphazard,
And unaccented:
To re-faith himself,
He rummages lines,
Plangent or pungent,
By bards of sentence,
But all to his sample
Ring fribble or fop,
Not one of them worth
A hangman's wages.

MOON LANDING

It's natural the Boys should whoop it up for
so huge a phallic triumph, an adventure
    it would not have occurred to women
    to think worth while, made possible only

because we like huddling in gangs and knowing
the exact time: yes, our sex may in fairness
    hurrah the deed, although the motives
    that primed it were somewhat less than *menschlich.*

A grand gesture. But what does it period?
What does it osse? We were always adroiter
    with objects than lives, and more facile
    at courage than kindness: from the moment

the first flint was flaked this landing was merely
a matter of time. But our selves, like Adam's,
    still don't fit us exactly, modern
    only in this—our lack of decorum.

Homer's heroes were certainly no braver
than our Trio, but more fortunate: Hector
    was excused the insult of having
    his valor covered by television.

Worth *going* to see? I can well believe it.
Worth *seeing*? Mneh! I once rode through a desert
    and was not charmed: give me a watered
    lively garden, remote from blatherers

about the New, the von Brauns and their ilk, where
on August mornings I can count the morning
    glories, where to die has a meaning,
    and no engine can shift my perspective.

Unsmudged, thank God, my Moon still queens the Heavens
as She ebbs and fulls, a Presence to glop at,
    Her Old Man, made of grit not protein,
    still visits my Austrian several

with His old detachment, and the old warnings
still have power to scare me: Hybris comes to
    an ugly finish, Irreverence
    is a greater oaf than Superstition.

Our apparatniks will continue making
the usual squalid mess called History:
    all we can pray for is that artists,
    chefs and saints may still appear to blithe it.

THE GARRISON

Martini-time: time to draw the curtains and
choose a composer we should like to hear from,
before coming to table for one of your
        savoury messes.

Time crumbs all ramparts, brachypod Nemesis
catches up sooner or later with hare-swift
Achilles, but personal song and language
        somehow mizzle them.

Thanks to which it's possible for the breathing
still to break bread with the dead, whose brotherhood
gives us confidence to wend the trivial
        thrust of the Present,

so self-righteous in its assumptions and so
certain that none dare out-face it. We, Chester,
and the choir we sort with have been assigned to
        garrison stations.

Whoever rules, our duty to the City
is loyal opposition, never greening
for the big money, never neighing after
a public image.

Let us leave rebellions to the choleric
who enjoy them: to serve as a paradigm
now of what a plausible Future might be
is what we're here for.

PSEUDO-QUESTIONS

Who could possibly approve of Metternich
and his Thought Police? Yet in a liberal
milieu would Adalbert Stifter have written
    his noble idylls?

Vice versa, what God-fearing Magistrate
would dream of shaking hands with a financial
crook and Anti-Semite? Yet Richard Wagner
    wrought masterpieces.

Wild horses could not drag me to debates on
Art and Society: critics with credos,
Christian or Marxist, should keep their trap shut,
    lest they spout nonsense.

STARK BEWÖLKT

for STELLA MUSULIN

I'm no photophil who burns
his body brown on beaches:
foolish I find this fashion
of modern surf-riding man.
Let plants by all means sun-bathe,
it helps them to make their meals,
exposure, through, to ultra-
-violet vapids the brain,
bids us be stodge and stupid.
Still, safe in some sheltered shade,
or watching through a window,
an ageing male, I demand
to see a smiling summer,
a sky bright and wholly blue,
save for a drifting cloudlet
like a dollop of whipped cream.
This year all is unthuswise:
O why so glum, weather-god?

Day after day we waken
to be scolded by a scowl,

venomous and vindictive,
a flat frowning Friday face,
horrid as a hang-over,
and mean as well: if you must
so disarray the heavens,
at least you might let them rain.
(Water is always welcome,
for trees to take neat and men
to make brandy or beer with.)
But, no, we don't get a drop,
dry you remain and doleful
in a perpetual pique.

Fowls mope, flowers are wretched,
the raspberry-canes are forced
into phyllomania.
To ignore you, not be cross,
one would have to be either
drunk, lit on amphetamines,
or a feverish lover:
being dead sober all day,
I find your bearing boorish,
by four in the afternoon
frequently close the curtains
to shut your shabbiness out.

Who or what are you mad at?
What has poor Austria done
to draw such disapproval?
The *Beamterei,* it's true,
is as awful as ever,
the drivers are dangerous,
standards at the *Staatsoper*
steadily decline each year,

and *Wien*'s become provincial
compared to the pride She was.
Still, it's a cosy country,
unracked by riots or strikes
and backward at drug-taking:
I've heard of a dozen lands
where life sounds far more ugsome,
fitter goals for your disgust.
(I needn't name them, for you, whose
glance circumspects the whole globe,
ken at first-hand what's cooking.)

Have done! What good does it do,
dumb god, just to deject us?
Foul our function may be, but
foul weather won't reform it.
If you merely wish our world
to mend its ways, remember:
when happy, men on the whole
behave a wee bit better,
when unhappy, always worse.

NATURAL LINGUISTICS

for PETER SALUS

Every created thing has ways of pronouncing its ownhood:
    basic and used by all, even the mineral tribes,
is the hieroglyphical *koine* of visual appearance
    which, though it lacks the verb, is, when compared with our own
heaviest lexicons, so much richer and subtler in shape-nouns,
    color-adjectives and apt prepositions of place.
Verbs first appear with the flowers who utter imperative odors
    which, with their taste for sweets, insects are bound to obey:
motive, too, in the eyes of beasts is the language of gesture
    (urban life has, alas, sadly impoverished ours),
signals of interrogation, friendship, threat and appeasement,
    instantly taken in, seldom, if ever, misread.
All who have managed to break through the primal barrier of Silence
    into an audible world find an indicative AM:
though some carnivores, leaving messages written in urine,
    use a preterite WAS, none can conceive of a WILL,
nor have they ever made subjunctive or negative statements,
    even cryptics whose lives hang upon telling a fib.
Rage and grief they can sing, not self-reproach or repentance,
    nor have they legends to tell, though their respect for a rite

is more pious than ours, for a complex code of releasers
    trains them to walk in the ways which their ur-ancestors trod.
(Some of these codes remain mysteries to us: for instance,
    fish who travel in huge loveless anonymous turbs,
what is it keeps them in line? Our single certainty is that
    minnows deprived of their fore-brains go it gladly alone.)
Since in their circles it's not good form to say anything novel,
    none ever stutter on *er,* guddling in vain for a word,
none are at loss for an answer: none, it seems, are bilingual,
    but, if they cannot translate, that is the ransom they pay
for just doing their thing, not greedily trying to publish
    all the world as we do into our picture at once.
If they have never laughed, at least they have never talked drivel,
    never tortured their own kind for a point of belief,
never, marching to war, inflamed by fortissimo music,
    hundreds of miles from home died for a verbal whereas.

"Dumb" we may call them but, surely, our poets are right in assuming
    all would prefer that they were rhetorized *at* than *about.*

THE ALIENS

for WILLIAM GRAY

Wide though the interrupt be that divides us, runers and counters,
from the Old World of the Plants, all lapped in a tolerant silence,
where, by the grace of chlorophyll, few of them ever have taken
life and not one put a sceptical question, we nod them as neighbours
who, to conclude from their friendly response to a gardener's handling,
like to be given the chance to get more than a self-education.
As for the hot-blooded Beasts, we didn't need Darwin to tell us
horses and rabbits and mice are our cognates, the double-voiced song-birds
cousins, however removed: unique as we seem, we, too, are
shovelled out into the cold, poodle-naked, as male or as female,
grab at and gobble up proteins, drop dung, perform the ungainly
brute-with-two-backs until, dared and doddered by age, we surrender,
lapse into stagnant stuff, while they by retaining a constant
visible shape through a lifetime, accord with our human idea of
having a Self. They also, we cannot but fancy, are peering
at a horizon as we do, aware of, however obscurely,
more than they must be concerned with, and vaguely elated at being

someone who's up and about: yes, even their humblest have, surely,
nosed a few steps on the hazardous foreright to courage
utterance, joy and collateral love. That is why, in our folk-tales,
toads and squirrels can talk, in our epics the great be compared to
lions or foxes or eagles.

                                     But between us and the Insects,
namely nine-tenths of the living, there grins a prohibitive fracture
empathy cannot transgress: (What Saint made a friend of a roach or
preached to an ant-hill?) Unrosed by a shame, unendorsed by a sorrow,
blank to a fear of failure, they daunt alike the believer's
faith in a fatherly providence and the atheist's dogma of purely
random events. To begin as a crawling insatiable eater,
then to be buried and mortify, then to emerge from the cere-cloth
winged and mateable, brilliantly coloured, a sipper of juices,
yet a compulsive hunter and hoarder, must do havoc to any
unitive sense. To insert them, excuse those unaimiable towns where
sex is reserved for the Few and the many animate tool-kits
perish from overwear, one is tempted to cook up a Gnostic
myth of an earlier Fall, preceding by aeons the Reptiles:
Adam, a crab-like creature who'd just wriggled out of a steamy
ocean where he had failed at making a living and now lay
moribund, choked, on a shore without song. Unto whom the Seducer,
not our romantic Satan but a clever cartesian Archon,
coaxingly thus: *Not doing very well, are you, poor deathling,*
no, and unlikely to do any better, thanks to the schemes of
We-Know-Whom. (He's a Precious but logic was never his forte.)
Freedom may manage in Heaven with Incorporeals, but for

ghosted extended matter the consequence is to be doomed to
err where an error is mortal. But trust me and live, for I do know
clearly what needs to be done. If I programme your ganglia for you,
you shall inherit the earth.

                              Such a myth, we all know, is no answer.
What they mean to themselves or to God is a meaningless question:
they to us are quite simply what we must never become.

DOGGEREL BY A SENIOR CITIZEN

for ROBERT LEDERER

Our earth in 1969
Is not the planet I call mine,
The world, I mean, that gives me strength
To hold off chaos at arm's length.

My Eden landscapes and their climes
Are constructs from Edwardian times,
When bath-rooms took up lots of space,
And, before eating, one said Grace.

The automobile, the aeroplane,
Are useful gadgets, but profane:
The enginery of which I dream
Is moved by water or by steam.

Reason requires that I approve
The light-bulb which I cannot love:
To me more reverence-commanding
A fish-tail burner on the landing.

34

My family ghosts I fought and routed,
Their values, though, I never doubted:
I thought their Protestant Work-Ethic
Both practical and sympathetic.

When couples played or sang duets,
It was immoral to have debts:
I shall continue till I die
To pay in cash for what I buy.

The Book of Common Prayer we knew
Was that of 1662:
Though with-it sermons may be well,
Liturgical reforms are hell.

Sex was, of course—it always is—
The most enticing of mysteries,
But news-stands did not yet supply
Manichaean pornography.

Then Speech was mannerly, an Art,
Like learning not to belch or fart:
I cannot settle which is worse,
The Anti-Novel or Free Verse.

Nor are those Ph.D's my kith,
Who dig the symbol and the myth:
I count myself a man of letters
Who writes, or hopes to, for his betters.

Dare any call Permissiveness
An educational success?
Saner those class-rooms which I sat in,
Compelled to study Greek and Latin.

Though I suspect the term is crap,
If there *is* a Generation Gap,
Who is to blame? Those, old or young,
Who will not learn their Mother-Tongue.

But Love, at least, is not a state
Either *en vogue* or out-of-date,
And I've true friends, I will allow,
To talk and eat with here and now.

Me alienated? Bosh! It's just
As a sworn citizen who must
Skirmish with it that I feel
Most at home with what is Real.

SHORTS I

A poet's hope: to be,
like some valley cheese,
local, but prized elsewhere.

* * *

A disappointed
politician, he became
obsessed in age with
the social virtues of rooks,
and adopted two leeches.

* * *

Who can picture
Calvin, Pascal or Nietzsche,
as a pink chubby boy?

* * *

Deprived of a mother to love him,
Descartes divorced
Mind from Matter.

* * *

When engineers drink together,
what professional
jokes can they tell?

* * *

The glass-lens
desanctified Sight: men believed
they had seen through Nature.

* * *

Space was holy to
pilgrims of old, till the plane
stopped all that nonsense.

* * *

When gales assault them,
trees are always astonished,
but never ask why.

* * *

The fire mumbles on
to itself, but allows us
to overhear it.

* * *

Rivers, sooner or later,
all reach some ocean,
and in due season all men
arrive at a death-bed, but
neither on purpose.

* * *

Youth, like the Press, is excited when Nature
throws one of her tantrums, but Age approves Her
when She's courteous: earthquakes, floods, eruptions,
  seem a bit vulgar.

  *   *   *

Our tables and chairs and sofas
Know things about us
our lovers can't.

  *   *   *

What we touch is always
an Other: I may fondle
my leg, not Me.

  *   *   *

In moments of joy
all of us wished we possessed
a tail we could wag.

  *   *   *

Why must Growth rob us
of the infant's heavenly
power to bellow?

  *   *   *

When I was little . . .
Why should this unfinished phrase
so pester me now?

  *   *   *

Who, upon hearing
a tape of his speaking voice,
is not revolted?

* * *

Their senses cannot
teach the tired: they can only
feel in general.

* * *

Oncers do no damage:
only those who could love
can really corrupt.

* * *

Only bad rhetoric
can improve this world:
to true Speech it is deaf.

* * *

The words of liars
blush, but a statistician's
figures are shameless.

* * *

Virtue is always
more expensive than Vice, but
cheaper than Madness.

* * *

Cosmic trivia
we all are, but none of us
are unessential.

* * *

What is Death? A Life
disintegrating into
smaller simpler ones.

* * *

It is the unimportant
who make all the din:
both God and the Accuser
speak very softly.

* * *

God never makes knots,
but is expert, if asked to,
at untying them.

* * *

Does God ever judge
us by appearances? I
suspect that He does.

* * *

THE BALLAD OF BARNABY

for CHUCK TURNER

(*to Guitar accompaniment*)
Listen, good people, and you shall hear
A story of old that will gladden your ear,
The Tale of Barnaby, who was, they say,
The finest tumbler of his day.

In every town great crowds he drew,
And all men marvelled to see him do
The French Vault, the Vault of Champagne,
The Vault of Metz, and the Vault of Lorraine.

His eyes were blue, his figure was trim,
He liked the girls and the girls liked him;
For years he lived a life of vice,
Drinking in taverns and throwing the dice.

It happened one day he was riding along
Between two cities, whistling a song,
When he saw what then was quite common to see,
Two ravens perched on a gallows-tree.

"Barnaby," the first raven began,
"Will one day be as this hanging man":
"Yes," said the other, "and we know well
That when that day comes he will go to Hell."

Then Barnaby's conscience smote him sore;
He repented of all he had done heretofore:
"Woe is me! I will forsake
This wicked world and penance make."

The evening air was grave and still
When he came to a monastery built on a hill:
As its bells the Angelus did begin,
He knocked at the door and they let him in.

(*Choral music*)
The monks in that place were men of parts,
Learned in the sciences and the arts:
The Abbot could logically define
The place of all creatures in the Scheme Divine.

Brother Maurice then wrote down all that he said
In a flowing script that it might be read,
And Brother Alexander adorned the book
With pictures that gave it a beautiful look.

There were brothers there who could compose
Latin Sequences in verse and prose,
And a brother from Picardy, too, who sung
The praise of Our Lady in the vulgar tongue.

(*Choral music*)
Now Barnaby had never learned to read,
Nor *Paternoster* knew nor *Creed;*
Watching them all at work and prayer,
Barnaby's heart began to despair.

Down to the crypt at massing-time
He crept like a man intent on crime:
In a niche there above the altar stood
A statue of Our Lady carved in wood.

"Blessed Virgin," he cried, "enthroned on high,
Ignorant as a beast am I:
Tumbling is all I have learnt to do;
Mother-of-God, let me tumble for You."

Straightway he stripped off his jerkin,
And his tumbling acts he did begin:
So eager was he to do Her honor
That he vaulted higher than ever before.

(*Ballet music*)
The French Vault, the Vault of Champagne,
The Vault of Metz and the Vault of Lorraine,
He did them all till he sank to the ground,
His body asweat and his head in a swound.

Unmarked by him, Our Lady now
Steps down from her niche and wipes his brow.
"Thank you, Barnaby," She said and smiled;
"Well have you tumbled for me, my child."

From then on at the Office-Hours
Barnaby went to pay Her his devoirs.
One brother thought to himself: "Now where
Does Barnaby go at our times of prayer?"

And so next day when Barnaby slipped
Away he followed him down to the crypt.
When he saw how he honored the Mother-of-God,
This brother thought: "This is very odd.

It may be well: I believe it is,
But the Abbot, surely, should know of this."
To the Abbot he went with reverent mien
And told him exactly what he had seen.

The Abbot said to him: "Say no word
To the others of what you have seen and heard.
I will come to-morrow and watch with you
Before I decide what I ought to do."

Next day behind a pillar they hid,
And the Abbot marked all that Barnaby did.
Watching him leap and vault and tumble,
He thought, "This man is holy and humble."

(Ballet music)
"Lady," cried Barnaby, "I beg of Thee
To intercede with Thy Son for me!",
Gave one more leap, then down he dropped,
And lay dead still, for his heart had stopped.

Then grinning demons, black as coal,
Swarmed out of Hell to seize his soul:
"In vain shall be his pious fuss,
For every tumbler belongs to us."

(Ballet music)
But Our Lady and Her angels held them at bay,
With shining swords they drove them away,
And Barnaby's soul they bore aloft,
Singing with voices sweet and soft.

Chorus: Gloria in excelsis Deo.

SHORTS II

How many ravishing things whose innocent beauty astounds us
    owe their existence to Greed, Fear or Vainglory or Guilt.

* * *

Lucky the poets of old; for half their work was done for them:
    all would applaud when they named places or heroes or gods.
Proper Names are *an-sich* poetic, but now there is hardly
    one that a poet will dare pen without adding a gloss.

* * *

Blessed be all metrical rules that forbid automatic responses,
    force us to have second thoughts, free from the fetters of Self.

* * *

No, Surrealists, no! No, even the wildest of poems
    must, like prose, have a firm basis in staid common-sense.

* * *

I suspect that without some undertone of the comic
    genuine serious verse cannot be written to-day.

47

* * *

What should I write at Sixty-Four? is a question, a folly
  What should I write in Nineteen-Hundred-and-Seventy-One?

* * *

To-day two poems begged to be written: I had to refuse them.
  Sorry, no longer, my dear! Sorry, my precious, not yet!

* * *

Like it is among all wild men and repetitive creatures,
  eyed from a singular stand-point, is the Why of the Arts.
Poet, employ your vocative talent to utter exactly
  what you were graced to behold: leave us to judge for ourselves.

* * *

Psychological critics, do be more precise in your language:
  symbols must not be confused with allegorical signs.

* * *

Shameless envious Age!, when the Public will shell out more cash for
  note-books and sketches that were never intended for them
than for perfected works. Observing erasures and blunders,
  every amateur thinks: *I could have done it as well.*

* * *

Gossip-Columnists I can forgive for they make no pretences,
  not Biographers who claim it's for Scholarship's sake.

* * *

Autobiographer, please don't tell me the tale of your love-life:
  much as it mattered to you, nothing could marvel me less.

* * *

Why is pornography boring? Because it can never surprise us.
    All of us know the few things Man as a mammal can do.

* * *

Knowing artists, you think that you know all about Prima Donnas:
    boy!, just wait till you hear scientists get up and sing.

* * *

Why should the cleverest minds so often hold the religion
    Sacred is any Machine, all that's alive is profane?

* * *

Those who run to the apes to explain our behaviour are chuckle-
    -heads too dumb to know their arse from a hole-in-the-ground.

* * *

If all our acts are conditioned behaviour, then so are our theories:
    yet your behaviourist claims his is objectively true.

* * *

Horse-Flies, why didn't Nature bring you up to respect us?
    Bite us you can, but it is usually fatal for you.

* * *

What we mean when we say that So-and-So's *a good person,*
    no psychologist can tell, for we certainly don't
mean that He has no problems: all that is clear is that, when we
    say this, nobody says, shaking his head—*He is bad!*

* * *

Talent calls for display, some public space to perform in:
    Virtue hills itself, even from virtuous men.

*   *   *

When two persons discover that they have a passion in common,
    Sex, Donizetti or Chows, Class is no barrier at all:
secret to every class, though, its code of polite conversation,
    how one should carry on when talking to strangers and bores.

*   *   *

Violence is never just, though Justice may sometimes require it:
    tyrants are persons to whom requisite evil is fun.

*   *   *

Alienation from the Collective is always a duty:
    every State is the Beast who is Estrangement itself.

*   *   *

Is it Progress when T.V.'s children know all the names
Of politicians, but no longer play children's games?

*   *   *

Yes, a Society so obsessed with rabid consumption
    stinks, I entirely agree: but, student radicals, why,
why protest in its own dehumanised language of Ad-Mass?
    if you would civil our land, first you should civil your speech.

*   *   *

Why strip naked and bellow words of four letters in public?
    Poor young things, can it be none of you have any friends?

*   *   *

Somebody shouted, I read: *We are ALL of us marvelously gifted!*
    Sorry, my love, but I am: You, though, have proved that You ain't.

* * *

In adolescence, of course, at times I was cross or unhappy,
    but I cannot recall once having ever been bored.

* * *

I'm for Freedom because I mistrust the Censor in office:
    but, if I held the job, my!, how severe I should be.

OLD PEOPLE'S HOME

All are limitory, but each has her own
nuance of damage. The elite can dress and decent themselves,
    are ambulant with a single stick, adroit
to read a book all through, or play the slow movements of
    easy sonatas. (Yet, perhaps their very
carnal freedom is their spirit's bane: intelligent
    of what has happened and why, they are obnoxious
to a glum beyond tears.) Then come those on wheels, the average
    majority, who endure T.V. and, led by
lenient therapists, do community-singing, then
    the loners, muttering in Limbo, and last
the terminally incompetent, as improvident,
    unspeakable, impeccable as the plants
they parody. (Plants may sweat profusely but never
    sully themselves.) One tie, though, unites them: all
appeared when the world, though much was awry there, was more
    spacious, more comely to look at, its Old Ones
with an audience and secular station. Then a child,

in dismay with Mamma, could refuge with Gran
to be revalued and told a story. As of now,
        we all know what to expect, but their generation
is the first to fade like this, not at home but assigned
        to a numbered frequent ward, stowed out of conscience
as unpopular luggage.
                        As I ride the subway
        to spend half-an-hour with one, I revisage
who she was in the pomp and sumpture of her hey-day,
        when week-end visits were a presumptive joy,
not a good work. Am I cold to wish for a speedy
        painless dormition, pray, as I know she prays,
that God or Nature will abrupt her earthly function?

CIRCE

Her Telepathic-Station transmits thought-waves
the second-rate, the bored, the disappointed,
and any of us when tired or uneasy,
    are tuned to receive.

So, though unlisted in atlas or phone-book,
her Garden is easy to find. In no time
one reaches the gate over which is written
    large: MAKE LOVE NOT WAR.

Inside it is warm and still like a drowsy
September day, though the leaves show no sign of
turning. All around one notes the usual
    pinks and blues and reds,

a shade over-emphasised. The rose-bushes
have no thorns. An invisible orchestra
plays the Great Masters: the technique is flawless,
    the rendering schmaltz.

Of Herself no sign. But, just as the pilgrim
is starting to wonder "Have I been hoaxed by
a myth?", he feels her hand in his and hears her
        murmuring: *At last!*

With me, mistaught one, you shall learn the answers.
What is Conscience but a nattering fish-wife,
the Tree of Knowledge but the splintered main-mast
        of the Ship of Fools?

Consent, you poor alien, to my arms where
sequence is conquered, division abolished:
soon, soon, in the perfect orgasm, you shall, pet,
        be one with the All.

She does not brutalise her victims (beasts could
bite or bolt), She simplifies them to flowers,
sessile fatalists who don't mind and only
        can talk to themselves.

All but a privileged Few, the elite She
guides to her secret citadel, the Tower
where a laugh is forbidden and DO HARM AS
        THOU WILT is the Law.

Dear little not-so-innocents, beware of
Old Grandmother Spider: rump her endearments.
She's not quite as nice as She looks, nor you quite
        as tough as you think.

SHORT ODE TO THE CUCKOO

No one now imagines you answer idle questions
—*How long shall I live? How long remain single?*
Will butter be cheaper?—nor does your shout make
    husbands uneasy.

Compared with arias by the great performers
such as the merle, your two-note act is kid-stuff:
our most hardened crooks are sincerely shocked by
    your nesting habits.

Science, Aesthetics, Ethics, may huff and puff but they
cannot extinguish your magic: you marvel
the commuter as you wondered the savage.
    Hence, in my diary,

where I normally enter nothing but social
engagements and, lately, the death of friends, I
scribble year after year when I first hear you,
    of a holy moment.

ODE TO THE MEDIEVAL POETS

Chaucer, Langland, Douglas, Dunbar, with all your
brother Anons, how on earth did you ever manage,
    without anaesthetics or plumbing,
      in daily peril from witches, warlocks,

lepers, The Holy Office, foreign mercenaries
burning as they came, to write so cheerfully,
    with no grimaces of self-pathos?
      Long-winded you could be but not vulgar,

bawdy but not grubby, your raucous flytings
sheer high-spirited fun, whereas our makers,
    beset by every creature comfort,
      immune, they believe, to all superstitions,

even at their best are so often morose or
kinky, petrified by their gorgon egos.
    We all ask, but I doubt if anyone
      can really say why all age-groups should find our

Age quite so repulsive. \ Without its heartless
engines, though, you could not tenant my book-shelves,
    on hand to delect my ear and chuckle
      my sad flesh: I would gladly just now be

turning out verses to applaud a thundery
jovial June when the judas-tree is in blossom,
    but am forbidden by the knowledge
      that you would have wrought them so much better.

AN ENCOUNTER

The Year: 452. The Place: the southern
bank of the River Po. The forelook: curtains
on further hopes of a Western and Christian
    civilisation.

For Attila and his Hun Horde, slant-eyed, sallow,
the creatures of an animist horse-culture,
dieted on raw-meat and goat-cheese, nocent to
    cities and letters.

were tented there, having routed the imperial
armies and preyed the luscious North, which now lay
frauded of mobile goods, old sedentary
    structures distorted.

Rome was ghastly. What earthly reason was there
why She should now not be theirs for the taking?
The Pope alone kept his cool, to the enemy
    now came in person,

sequenced by psalm-singing brethren: astonished,
Attila stared at a manner of men so
unlike his. "Your name?", he snapped at their leader.
       "Leo," he answered, raising

his right hand, the forefinger pointed upwards,
the little finger pressed to the thumb, in the
Roman salute: "I ask the King to receive me
       in private audience."

Their parley was held out of earshot: we only
know it was brief, that suddenly Attila
wheeled his horse and galloped back to the encampment,
       yelling out orders.

Next morning the site was vacant: they had vanished,
never to vex us again. What can Leo have
actually said? He never told, and the poets
       can only imagine

speeches for those who share a common cosmos:
all we can say is that he rose to the occasion,
that for once, and by His own standards, the Prince of
       this world showed weakness.

A SHOCK

Housman was perfectly right.
Our world rapidly worsens:
nothing now is so horrid
or silly it can't occur.
Still, I'm stumped by what happened
to upper-middle-class me,
born in '07, that is,
the same time as *Elektra,*
gun-shy myopic grandchild
of Anglican clergymen,
suspicious of all passion,
including passionate love,
day-dreaming of leafy dells
that shelter carefree shepherds,
averse to violent weather,
pained by the predator beasts,
shocked by boxing and blood-sports,
when I, I, I, if you please,
at Schwechat Flughafen was
frisked by a cop for weapons.

ANTHEM

Let us praise our Maker, with true passion extol Him.
Let the whole creation give out another sweetness,
Nicer in our nostrils, a novel fragrance
From cleansed occasions in accord together
As one feeling fabric, all flushed and intact,
Phenomena and numbers announcing in one
Multitudinous oecumenical song
Their grand givenness of gratitude and joy,
Peaceable and plural, their positive truth
An authoritative This, an unthreatened Now
When, in love and in laughter, each lives itself,
For, united by His Word, cognition and power,
System and Order, are a single glory,
And the pattern is complex, their places safe.

UNITED NATIONS HYMN

(Music by Pablo Casals)

Eagerly, Musician,
Strike your string,
So we may sing,
Elated, Optative,
Our several voices
Interblending,
Playfully contending,
Not interfering
But co-inhering,
For all within
The cincture of the sound
Is holy ground,
Where all are Brothers,
None faceless Others.

Let mortals beware
Of words, for
With words we lie,
Can say peace when we mean war,
Foul thought speak fair

And promise falsely.
But song is true:
Let music for peace
Be the paradigm,
For peace means to change
At the right time,
As the World-Clock
Goes tick and tock.

So may the story
Of our human city
Presently move
Like music, when
Begotten notes
New notes beget,
Making the flowing
Of time a growing,
Till what it could be
At last it is,
Where even sadness
Is a form of gladness,
Where Fate is Freedom,
Grace and Surprise.

NOTE: Some of the lines in the last stanza I wrote for a Canadian Film Board
Documentary, Long Distance Runner. I found I needed them again.

TO GOETHE: A COMPLAINT

How wonderfully your songs begin
With praise of Nature and her beauty,
But then, as if it were a duty,
You drag some god-damned sweetheart in.
Did you imagine she'd be flattered?
They never sound as if they mattered.

CONTRA BLAKE

The Road of Excess
leads, more often than not, to
The Slough of Despond.

A TOAST

to PROFESSOR WILLIAM EMPSON
on the occasion of his retirement in 1971

As *quid pro quo* for your enchanting verses,
when approached by Sheffield, at first I wondered
if I could manage *Just a Smack at Empson,*
    but nothing occurred.

All I could fault was your conceit that Milton's
God, obtrusive prolix baroque Olympian,
is our Christian one. Who, though, but you has pondered
    so deeply on *Alice?*

Good voices are rare, still rarer singers with
perfect pitch: if Graves was right, if at Cambridge
the tuning's a wee bit sharp, then at Oxford
    it well may be flat.

Our verbal games are separate, thank heaven,
but Time twins us: both learned to person Life in
an open-hearthed, nannied, un-T-V'd world, where
    cars looked peculiar.

To wish you long long years would be heartless (may you
leave when you want to, no earlier) : but I gladly,
dear Bill, dear fellow mandarin, smile to your
        future holidays.

LONELINESS

Gate-crashing ghost, aggressive
invisible visitor,
tactless gooseberry, spoiling
my *tête-à-tête* with myself,
blackmailing brute, behaving
as if the house were your own,
so viciously pursuing
your victim from room to room,
monotonously nagging,
ungenerous jabberer,
dirty devil, befouling
fair fancies, making the mind
a quagmire of disquiet,
weakening my will to work,
shadow without shape or sex,
excluding consolation,
blotting out Nature's beauties,
grey mist between me and God,
pestilent problem that won't

be put on the back-burner,
hard it is to endure you.

Routine is the one technique
I know of that enables
your host to ignore you now:
while typing business letters,
laying the table for one,
gobbling a thoughtless luncheon,
I briefly forget you're there,
but am safe from your haunting
only when soundly asleep.

History counsels patience:
tyrants come, like plagues, but none
can rule the roost for ever.
Indeed, your totter is near,
your days numbered: to-morrow
Chester, my chum, will return.
Then you'll be through: in no time
he'll throw you out neck-and-crop.
We'll merry-make your cadence
with music, feasting and fun.

TALKING TO DOGS

IN MEMORIAM ROLFI STROBL
Run over, June 9th, 1970

From us, of course, you want gristly bones
and to be led through exciting odorscapes
        —their colors don't matter—with the chance
of a rabbit to chase or of meeting
        a fellow arse-hole to snuzzle at,
but your deepest fury is to be accepted
        as junior members of a Salon
suaver in taste and manners than a pack,
        to be scratched on the belly and talked to.
Probably, you only hear vowels and then only if
        uttered with lyrical emphasis,
so we cannot tell you a story, even
        when it is true, nor drily dissect
in the third person neighbors who are not there
        or things which can't blush. And what do we,
those of us who are householders, not shepherds
        or killers or polar explorers,
ask from you? The admiration of creatures
        to whom mirrors mean nothing, who never
false your expression and so remind us

that we as well are still social retards,
who have never learned to command our feelings
and don't want to, really. Some great men,
Goethe and Lear, for instance, have disliked you,
which seems eccentric, but good people,
if they keep one, have good dogs. (The reverse
is not so, for some very bad hats
handle you very well.) It's those who crave
a querulous permanent baby,
or a little detachable penis,
who can, and often do, debase you.
Humor and joy to your thinking are one,
so that you laugh with your whole body,
and nothing dismays you more than the noise
of our local superior titters.
(But then our young males are dismayed by yours
to whom, except when a bitch is air-borne,
chastity seems to present no problem.)
Being quicker to sense unhappiness
without having to be told the dreary
details or who is to blame, in dark hours
your silence may be of more help than many
two-legged comforters. In citizens
obedience is not always a virtue,
but yours need not make us uneasy
because, though child-like, you are complete, no New
Generation whom it's our duty
to disappoint since, until they notice
our failings, they will never bother
to make their own mistakes. Let difference
remain our bond, yes, and the one trait
both have in common, a sense of theatre.

TALKING TO MICE

Plural the verdicts we cast on the creatures we have to shake hands with:
Creepy! Get HER! Good Lord, what an oddity! One to steer clear of!
Fun! Impossible! Nice, but a bore! An adorable monster!
But those animates which we call in our arrogance *dumb* are
judged as a species and classed by the melodramatic division,
either *Goodies* or *Baddies.* So spiders and roaches and flies we
excommunicate as—ugh!—all irredeemably evil,
Dreck to be stamped on or swatted, abolished without any hover.
Mice, *per contra,* except to a few hysterical women,
rank among the most comely of all the miniature mammals
who impinge on our lives, for our smell doesn't seem to alarm them,
visitors whom we can jump with, co-agents it doesn't seem phoney
we should endow with a *You,* as from now on I shall in these verses,
though my grammatical shift will be out of your ken for, alas, you
never have managed, as all successful parasites must, to
crack the code of your host, wise up on what habits can travel.

Ah!, if only you had, with what patience we would have trained you
how to obtemper your greeds, recalling the way that our Nannies
moulded our nursery *moeurs,* bechiding whenever we turned our
noses up at a dish—*Now remember the starving Armenians!*—

and when we gobbled—*Enough! Leave something for nice Mr. Manners!*—
cited you suitable maxims. *Good Little Mice never gnaw through*
wood-work or nibble at packages. Good Little Mice never scatter
droppings that have to be swept up. Good Little Mice get a tid-bit,
Bad Little Mice die young. Then, adapting an adage of lovers,
Two Little Mice are a company, Three Little Mice are a rabble.

All through the Spring and the Summer, while you were still only a couple,
fit-sides we dwelt in a peace as idyllic as only a Beatrix
Potter could paint. In September, though, this was abrupted: you must have
littered for, lo! quite suddenly, there were a swarm of you, messing
everything up until no cache was aloof to your insults.
What occurred now confirmed that ancient political axiom:
When Words fail to persuade, then Physical Force gives the orders.
Knowing you trusted in us, and would never believe an unusual
object pertaining to men could be there for a sinister purpose,
traps were baited and one by one you were fatally humbugged.
All fourteen of you perished. To move from where we'd been sipping
cocktails and giving ear, translated out of ourselves, to
Biedermeyer Duets or Strauss in *Metamorphosen,*
mourning the end of his world, and enter the kitchen to find there
one more broken cadaver, its black eyes beadily staring,
obumbated a week. We had felt no talent to murder,
it was against our pluck. Why, why then? For *raisons d'État*. As
householders we had behaved exactly as every State does,
when there is something It wants, and a minor one gets in the way.

73

TALKING TO MYSELF

for O L I V E R   S A C K S

Spring this year in Austria started off benign,
the heavens lucid, the air stable, the about
sane to all feeders, vegetate or bestial:
the deathless minerals looked pleased with their regime,
where what is not forbidden is compulsory.

Shadows of course there are, Porn-Ads, with-it clergy,
and hubby next door has taken to the bottle,
but You have preserved your poise, strange rustic object,
whom I, made in God's Image but already warped,
a malapert will-worship, must bow to as Me.

My mortal manor, the carnal territory
allotted to my manage, my fosterling too.
I must earn cash to support, my tutor also,
but for whose neural instructions I could never
acknowledge what is or imagine what is not.

Instinctively passive, I guess, having neither
fangs nor talons nor hooves nor venom, and therefore
too prone to let the sun go down upon your funk,
a poor smeller, or rather a censor of smells,
with an omnivore palate that can take hot food.

Unpredictably, decades ago, You arrived
among that unending cascade of creatures spewed
from Nature's maw. A random event, says Science.
Random my bottom! A true miracle, say I,
for who is not certain that he was meant to be?

As You augmented and developed a profile,
I looked at your looks askance. *His architecture
should have been much more imposing: I've been let down!*
By now, though, I've gotten used to your proportions
and, all things considered, I might have fared far worse.

Seldom have You been a bother. For many years
You were, I admit, a martyr to horn-colic
(it did no good to tell You—*But I'm not in love!*):
how stoutly, though, You've repelled all germ invasions,
but never chastised my tantrums with a megrim.

You are the Injured Party for, if short-sighted,
I am the book-worm who tired You, if short-winded
as cigarette addicts are, I was the pusher
who got You hooked. (Had we been both a bit younger,
I might well have mischiefed You worse with a needle.)

I'm always amazed at how little I know You.
Your coasts and outgates I know, for I govern there,
but what goes on inland, the rites, the social codes,
your torrents, salt and sunless, remain enigmas:
what I believe is on doctors' hearsay only.

Our marriage is a drama, but no stage-play where
what is not spoken is not thought: in our theatre
all that I cannot syllable You will pronounce
in acts whose *raison-d'être* escapes me. Why secrete
fluid when I dole, or stretch your lips when I joy?

Demands to close or open, include or eject,
must come from your corner, are no province of mine
(all I have done is to provide the time-table
of hours when You may put them): but what is your work
when I librate between a glum and a frolic?

For dreams I, quite irrationally, reproach You.
All I know is that I don't choose them: if I could,
they would conform to some prosodic discipline,
mean just what they say. Whatever point nocturnal
manias make, as a poet I disapprove.

Thanks to your otherness, your jocular concords,
so unlike my realm of dissonance and anger,
You can serve me as my emblem for the Cosmos:
for human congregations, though, as Hobbes perceived,
the apposite sign is some ungainly monster.

Whoever coined the phrase *The Body Politic?*
All States we've lived in, or historians tell of,
have had shocking health, psychosomatic cases,
physicked by sadists or glozing expensive quacks:
when I read the papers, You seem an Adonis.

Time, we both know, will decay You, and already
I'm scared of our divorce: I've seen some horrid ones.
Remember: when *Le Bon Dieu* says to You *Leave him!*,
please, please, for His sake and mine, pay no attention
to my piteous *Dont*'s, but bugger off quickly.

ABOUT THE AUTHOR

MR. AUDEN is the author of several volumes of poetry including *About the House, Homage to Clio, The Double Man, For the Time Being, The Age of Anxiety, Nomes, The Shield of Achilles,* and with Louis MacNeice, *Letters from Iceland* (reissued by Random House in 1969). His *Selected Poetry* appears in the Modern Library. New editions of *The Orators* and *Collected Shorter Poems* were published in 1967. *Collected Longer Poems* was published in 1969. *The Enchafèd Flood,* three critical essays on the romantic spirit, and a volume of essays, *The Dyer's Hand,* are available in Vintage Books. His most recent volume of essays is *Secondary Worlds.*

Mr. Auden has been the recipient of a number of awards, among them the Pulitzer Prize, the National Book Award, the Bollingen Prize for Poetry, the Guinness Poetry Award and, in 1967, the National Medal for Literature given by the National Book Committee.

Born in York, England, in 1907, Mr. Auden has been a resident of the United States since 1939 and an American citizen since 1946. While at school in England he became associated with Stephen Spender and Christopher Isherwood, who were to be recognized as the most promising of the new generation in English letters. He collaborated with Isherwood on several plays, including *The Dog Beneath the Skin* and *The Ascent of F-6* (available as *Two Great Plays* in Vintage Books).

His most recent book is *Academic Graffiti.*